My Maverick Muse

A Book of Poems

Nidhi Rana

BookLeaf Publishing

India | USA | UK

Made with ❤ on the BookLeaf Publishing Platform
www.bookleafpub.in
www.bookleafpub.com

Dedication

To every kindred soul
that sees
and finds its heart astir...

Preface

I think I have always loved words, not the spoken word though, just the written one. I am one of those quieter ones who observe and look into things, deconstructing them to tiny bits, that sometimes can be digested, and sometimes just chewed and discarded. My thoughts may sometimes have digressed from the conformist, conventional paths, hence the 'Maverick' in me, whose 'Muse' is everything to everyone. I may have failed miserably at times, but I have never stopped trying, and that is what makes me 'Me'.

I hope you enjoy the maverick and her muse!

Happy Reading!!

Acknowledgements

I am grateful to all those who have always stood by me, sometimes supporting, at other times just bearing with the maverick in me. I am thankful to God for creating me with this spark and blessing me with the spirit that has kept it kindled. I am highly indebted to the Book Leaf Publishers for presenting the opportunity to bring these random thoughts together as an anthology.

And, I am greatly obliged to you dear reader, for this book would mean nothing without you.

Thank you so much!!

To Be or Not to Be

Standing at the precipice
of my existence
I feel split
like Hamlet's dilemma-
To be or not to be!

My daughter,
her fever soaring,
pleads with silent eyes
wanting me to stay
to not go,
but duty calls.

I shut her image
in a loving corner
of my heart,
and stone-cold
enter the bank, and
sit at my desk,
with a smile

my eyes betray,
working the job
I need to work.

But do I not love her?

I open my laptop
She questions from her picture
as the screensaver.
I regret
leaving her with the maid.

This scourge of motherhood,
this little piece of my flesh and blood,
agonises me,
eats my heart out,
stops me from moving ahead.
The seed of discontent
thrives within me,
I am the Prometheus,
who must give the fire to humanity
and be eaten each day.

And I question endlessly-
'To be or not to be??'"

The Waiting Womb

The cat yowls
in the middle of the night
waking me up
with sweat under my skin
and blood between my legs.

I cry inside
and clean me up
thinking of the bird
who
on its return home
finds its nest fallen
and eggs broken-
Life snuffed out of them
A present and a future lost.

But the bird shrieks and hovers
for a while
above its loss
and flies to another tree

to build another nest
and start anew.
While I weep silently
sitting on the same barren bed
as my womb waits
to bring forth a new life.

Perhaps we aren't really same!
The bird is empowered
and I am not!

The Man and The Poet

The man scoffed
between his chuckles
and said,
'So, you are a poet,
a man of words.
But words are wind,
nonsensical burst,
a waste,
cast aside.
It is what man
cannot keep inside.'

The Poet said,
'Burst it is
but from the heart,
overflowing with
psychedelic emotions
felt deeper within
viscera of my being.
I comprehend

what confuses you.
It's your fear
of my ability to unearth
that
which is hidden
behind your words,
So, you speak thus.'

The man remarked,
'You are a dreamer.
What you write
is nothing
but
your half-crazed
imaginings
of all
that isn't real.'

The poet said,
'These dreams
are the space
where
all great ideas are born.
Even God had to dream
to get the idea
of creation of this world.'

The man angrily,
'Are you comparing
yourself to God?
You should be punished
for such ignominy.'

The poet laughed,
'To be able to see
what you cannot
and feel it all
deep inside my being,
is in itself a punishment.
But do it
if you may.
I cannot stop this-
It's His gift to me.'

And the dialogue has
been going on for ages,
one full of contempt
with an exaggerated self-worth,
and the other deferential
with a self-effacing spirit.

Stillness

The table,
the cup of coffee
and the silence
that soothes my ears.

Alone,
like an egret
on its one-legged perch,
I sit meditating,
conversing face-to-face
with myself.
I twist thoughts into shape
and ruminate over
the story of
rain and sunshine
in my life.

My silence makes people doubt me
for a weisenheimer,
see it as a pretense,

an obnoxious conceit,
but they do not know
that to hear the music
inside your heart,
stillness is a must.

The Real Woman

Her old skin
under the scanner
and dismissed
for age
from attention.

She prepares to go
under the knife
tighten the sags
uplift the jowls
smoothen the crow's feet,
a metal plate
invade her innards
and she becomes a silica doll
you can touch and mould
at will.

She has known
what it is to be desired
but desire isn't what she seeks.

She needs real love
and to feel loved,
A real man?

Or may be
She just needs to find
the real woman
inside of her
who loves
her cubbyholes,
her imperfections,
her marks of age,
and wear them as mementoes
of golden sunshine,
of numerous songs,
and untold tales,
of her years
loved and well-lived!

Her Lissome Smile

She walked cocksure
showering lissome smile
on the woman ahead.

Despite herself,
her eyes go down
to the woman's belly
distending conspicuously
under her *dupatta*
round, pregnant, fertile.

She sighed
cringing within
for the fecundity
that has eluded her.

Condemned by the world
for something
she cannot control,
her plight such.

She questions
her worth
and her womb
but not the world
for its inane cruelty.

Her lissome smile
soaked now
with despondent gloom.

(*dupatta*- a long piece of cloth worn around the head,
neck and shoulders by women from South Asia)

Stardust

Aren't we the dust-
cosmic and eternal,
that forms this universe?

We're the atoms-
primitive and original,
that God flung into space.
We exploded,
expanded, proliferated,
into stars and galaxies.
We were there
before the earth was born.
The atoms of hope we are!
A small grain of purpose
that strives and wriggles its way
into the womb of genesis;
We're the secret of conception,
infinite energies,
unfurling at each step, every chance,
breeding new worlds into being.

We're the dreamchasers.
We're the creators.
We're the miracles.
We are the throbbing life.
We're the stardust.

Sip by Sip

The Cafe
heady with aroma
of fresh-ground Cocoa
wafted the air.

The lost youth
with unshackled glee on display-
elemental, allied to,
the din of the Coffee Bar.
Their emotions liberated,
twirled in psychedelic dances
in the caffeinated clouds
over their cups of
espressos, mochas, lattes,
flat whites,
loaded with crème
insignificant, banal, cliché.

And she
in the corner

with her classic Café au lait
and salt and pepper hair
seemed strange
in that young Bistro.

Invisible to
the crowd drugged with coffee,
her wise eyes
ruminated over the numberless coffees
and her 'French Pressed' years
medium to the occasional 'Dark Roasts'
from her youth to age
significant and trivial
and she measured it all,
sip by sip,
slow, very slow!

I Meet the Night

I meet the night
lured by a symphony
that sings of
dreams and nightmares,
of ambitions and complacence,
of desires unspoken
left lying in a slumber.
Time moves,
moon floats,
stars sparkle,
trees creak,
leaves rustle,
owl hoots,
crickets whistle
shadows lurk,
darkness chases,
distant stream gurgles
as it gathers water
to fall into the sea,
and the night grows deeper.

Its choir-
delectable, melodic, portentous,
heavy with expectation
of the unknown.
I meet the night
with silence,
the silence inside of me.

On Forgetting

After a while
it's like nothing really ever happened
and if you speak of it,
it is you
who is bringing it to life.

Instead
you prefer not to speak
and
these moments full of dread
and embarrassment
become more distanced from imagination
vanishing from mind
impassable,
almost,
to ever have been real.

In the recesses of mind
hidden even to your own self
you wish it out of existence.

But have you really succeeded
in making it disappear,
dissipate into thin air,
like it never happened.

Can you remember something,
you have worked so hard
on forgetting?

New World

It rains
words and photos
and stories
these days
from the i-clouds
full with data
of a made-up world
retrieved in fake snippets,
provocative memes,
short reels,
and a life never lived,
assessed on a yardstick
of likes, comments
and little red hearts-
not beating,
but dead.

An Old Book

Have you ever felt the nostalgia
that clings to the yellow, brittle,
dog-eared pages of an old book?

On its frayed edges, have you felt
the warm touch of the hands
that once turned its pages?

Have you smelt the aroma of
the breath that instilled life
into its numberless stories?

Have you seen the silverfish
living inside those ancient pages
and chew on its wisdom?

I wonder at its held history,
lost forever,
as it lies invisible, unsold,
at a second-hand Bookstore?

From Book to Kindle

Moving on
from the book
to kindle
in a worthless bid
to adapt
to technology,
to learn the ways
of the new world,
I rant to my daughter-
of the old-world charm,
of the long halls of libraries,
of the musty smell rising
from books
with numerous wormholes,
of the feel of
yellow, gritty, brittle pages
of vintage classics
issued
from the state library.
And I deliver my tirade

against all this and more
while she sits glued to an iPad,
her outgrown appendage
it seems,
and to my utter dismay
the Bluetooth device
plugged into her ears.

Siesta

The long lazy fingers
of the hot summer noon
work their way
and like the sleeping beauty
pricked by the spindle
of her spinning wheel,
she falls asleep,
under the dark shade
of the gnarled mango tree,
in a nest
hidden in the hollows of trees,
in a crib
inside the pink nursery,
nodding by the window
on a mahogany armchair,
or snoozing on a mobile
by my pillow.
The languorous warmth,
the stillness of air,
the sluggish calm,

soothes her senses
making her lids heavy
sending her off
to hand pick the dreams
from the meadows of slumber,
during the quiet
of a siesta.

To Love a Man

To love a man
is a task so exhausting
that you must
forget your own being
and be the woman
who disappears
in an eclipse
like the moon
into non-being,
fulfilling him.
And like a God
He sits atop the hill
in his shrine
irate or happy
with your offerings
as he deems fit.
Fancy him
Worship him
Pray to him
Or love him

as you ought to,
But he will never
break through his halo
and meet you at the foothill
like the man that he must.

The History of Loss

Today,
Someone asked
If I had ever incurred a loss
to write of it so.

'Loss of someone', she specified.
Without much thought,
I nodded
and walked away.

But later
I thought of what she had asked.
and I questioned,
'Would the loss of smaller things
be not a loss at all?'

I have decried loss
so many times-
Loss of an earring
gifted on my wedding

by mum
after she's no more
to compensate.
Would it not be akin to
the loss of my mum itself,
once again?

Loss of the number of a long-lost friend
I bumped into
by chance
in the plaza
and he hurriedly scrawled
on a piece of paper
to keep in touch
and revive the friendship
blurred over time.
Wouldn't the loss of that paper
be a lost incurred twice?

And for that matter,
loss of trivia-
Favorite footwears outside the temple,
A letter that never found its way to you
through the letter boxes,
Loss of childhood,
Loss of youth,
Loss of words at a moment

you really need to speak your heart
because you might never see him again.

Losses make their own history-
A history of silences, absences,
omissions, gaps.
They are the lacunae of blanks
that keep staring at you
and
your life
keeps adding
into its inventory
slowly, steadily,
quite effortlessly!

The Journey

Expanse of the sky
burgeoning
brimming with turbid clouds
that threaten
to fall any moment,
drench me
soak my soul.

Far across
lining the horizon,
I see
the silhouette of
the lofty mountains.

There's the elusive road
snaking through the civilization,
that calls me
to keep moving forth,
to endure
to explore

to continue the quest
to find
my own true self
yet unknown to me.

And then,
there is my mind,
minding me
into safety,
to shun the thought
of exploration,
inducing into me
the fear of facing
the new,
saving my heart
of excess.

But also,
there's my heart
ready to break open
the shackles of
a secure life,
a life doomed
to be uneventful.
My heart
is feverish with
an exuberance of imagination,

stoked to discover
the primal,
untouched,
original
'Me'.

I am your Sky

Order isn't me
I am chaos.

Trying to find meaning in-
-the sun that rises
to colour me
in hues of yellow and red,
-the prick-pointed stars
that gaze back at me
on dark somber nights,
-the haze of the clouds
which covers as a veil
to later fall in madness
of a torrential rain,
-the tempestuous wind
that impels
to take me along
in spate of its anger.

I am the archive

of your obstinate hopes,
of your defiant dreams.
I am your imagination,
the fractious vision,
that makes you pick
one piece of
my muddled being
and
trim it into coherence.

I am your sky,
the vault of your being.

The Forest

She stood
with her eyes closed
and arms open,
extending herself
to take everything in,
while the forest
breathed around her
like a colossal being,
ready to enwrap her,
speaking to her
in a mother's whisper
soothing,
sedating,
in its own
language of quiet.

She saw the mists shift,
She heard the air speak!

The verduran musk

carried her
into the whirlpools,
a swirling maelstrom
of a vanished knowledge
of an ancient life
lived and forgotten
long long ago.

She grew through the roots,
into the branches,
flowering inside red blooms,
becoming the forest.

The Pine Cone

The pine cone,
happily detached
from its branch
Thuds!
Then, begins
to roll down the hill.
Whoosh!
It jumps
atop the rhododendron
blooming with red.
Swish!
It scratches through
the olive-green bush
full of thorns.
Plop!
It falls
into the brook
that spouted
ages hence
from behind

the ancient oak.

The cone
danced and sang
bobbed and bathed
in the clear waters
rapturous
in its freedom
till the day
it was plucked out
by someone
and painted
in bright colours
to adorn
the mantelpiece
above the fireplace
of his home.

He had Wings

The tiny beetle thought,
the leaf was its world.
He ate and he slept.
but the dreams
had disturbed him.
As he looked from the edges
of his planet,
he thought many thoughts,
The dreams kept coming back to him
and he questioned in silence,
'What if I jumped off?
Would I die?
Would I discover an alien land?
Would I fall through a bottomless chasm
and keep falling forever?'

He didn't know then,
that
He had wings!

The Mountain

The mountain
now bare
and brown
and benumbed,
stood silently
enduring
the mirage of life.
Its peace drowned
by the disorienting orchestra
of hammering sounds,
and pounding noises
of human activity
blasting
its pristine quiet.

Where is the course
of the rivulet
which rose near its crest?
Where have the birds
disappeared,

who sang primal songs?
Why the flowing branches
of ancient pines
have dried up
which forever kept
the sun from
touching the ground?

For now,
the mountain stands,
its soul parched,
but,
only he knows
till when
can he keep
the avalanche away
that lingers
near the snow line
impatient,
to wash the cacophony away,
till when can it smother
the tremors
gurgling in its bowels
from burying this
murderous civilization.

The Pine Forest

The mist
and the tall pine trees
that canopy the forest floor
envelop the woods
in a mystery unspoken.

The distant sound
of the shepherd's flute
haunts
echoing through the trees
singing through the pine needles
falling with the seeds
from inside the cones;
surreal,
the scenery,
hanging in the air,
like a strange dream,
that eclipses reason.

Is it the magic

of the old witch,
from the stories my mother told,
the enchantress
who casts her spell
and now sleeps snoring
in a cave
at the foot of the hill?

Meeting the Red God

I dragooned my feet
up the slope
to meet the Red God
who stood towering
upon the hill
among the pines.

His hand raised in benevolent blessing,
his all-seeing eyes
taking in the human notoriety
spread in a vast civilization
in front of him,
his weapon resting by his side,
lest he should be forced
to wield it.

I trudged through the ascent
to pray
to this mighty God,
that he rips my masks off

exorcise the shadows I host
make me cast my scales off
to bequeath me
with a skin
that renders my holes visible
such that
I could see myself as I.

But he stands quietly
in meditation,
willing me to face myself
on my own,
without his aid,
but deriving strength
from his presence,
the temple bells toll
ringing in the air,
and I stand
with my folded hands
tearing inside,
giving birth
to another me.

Silence

There is something beautiful
in silence.
The silence of a misty forest before dawn,
the stillness of the garden at noon,
or perhaps the hush after the storm,
or the quietness before it pours,
the shush of a country road at night,
the silence of desert under the hot sun,
the lull of reticence,
the quietness of the smoke
blending into the coldness of
a winter morning,
the mesmerizing quietness
of shadows in the hot sun,
the content of the lovers
when they have peaked and ebbed
in their love making,
the buttoned-up restraint
that mushrooms in nostalgia. . .

Silence draws a thin line
between
knowing and not knowing,
the here and now, and the after
the beginning and ending
of being and non-being.

Rain

Rain brings home
the fragrance
of childhood memories
whisked with petrichor
making me
melt into the drops of rain,
to fall in a mad hurry,
gather inside the womb
of earth,
stay,
become it,
run through the roots
of all alike,
the plants,
the animals,
the humans,
all,
run through their sinews,
and live it for a lifetime,
evaporate,

fall,
to live again
like the child
I once had been.

What lies Inside

I am scared to write
for the words reveal
what lies inside me
hidden.

It is the darkness
I have kept camouflaged
in the shadows
of my small being.
It is crooked and twisted
like the crags
by the Great Escarpment,
and the fathomless gorges
labyrinthine,
dangerous,
that could easily bring one
to her death.

Would that it were
a snowy mountain peak,

smooth and sunny,
I could dream to summit some day,
and show it off to the world!!

Continuum of Disappointments

My loneliness laments
in petty grumbles
and trite moans
that he brushes aside
dexterously
naming it
an anticipated petulance
a deficiency of character.
I grieve,
what he thinks of me,
but with restraint,
anguishing,
blundering my way
to his sardonic smiles.
Was it not meant
to be a togetherness?
A match made in heaven?
A marriage of the souls?

With heaviness,
I think of the
seven circumambulations
around the sacred fire,
seven lives to look forward to.

Huh!
Would there be
a hiatus
in the continuum
of disappointments?

Lost in the City

The city
in labyrinthine prints
makes me forget
the straight roads
to the sun
in the sky.

I remain lost
in the daze
of the fallen dust
on the dark streets
leading to
the line of dingy houses
where
I take a torn shelter,
halting and hesitant.

The yellow of my hope
gone ochre in disappointment,
the cyan of my belief

turned grey in self-doubt,
I have been everywhere
only to reach dead-ends.

I shall ask the flowing wind
to lend the blue of my longing
to the sky,
and take my auburn love
to the sun,
which,
should they accept,
would let me shine through them.

Alas!
Liberation from the gloom of this city.

Us

My daughters and I
rushed into the panting storm
and rode upon the sighing wind
borne on our brooms.

We were the rivers of light,
in black of the night
our hair, the mane of a lioness.

Gushing in aeolian tones
the squall hit us, and
the tempest tormented.

With battered bodies
and soaring spirits,
we howled with might
above the clamour of gale
raising a hurricane
out of ourselves,
and arrived

at the edge
of the precipice.

There,
between rocks and cold weather
we lit the sacred fire,
and danced into the night
to the hum of the universe,
singing songs of wisdom
to the Great Mother.

Dear Mother

Dear Mother,

You are my sun
I can hold and kiss,
but why
have you started
to burn me now?
Why have you started
dictating to me
the norms
of this creaking world
heavy with crimson insinuations?
The ivory song
you had sung to me
burnished in blaring heat
has lived in me,
and is branching out
with beautiful blooms.
I want to hum it
to my daughters now.

Please don't try
and mould me
into a cast
you've so wanted to disown.
Don't be bowed down
into a withered tree
at this juncture,
but be my spring
of new possibilities,
a riot of wings
over winds and waves.
Be my strength,
and my light,
that'd show me the path
out of every darkness,
out of this black hole
ready to engulf me.
I refuse
to be devoured
by this pain
that has ravaged you
and made you dwell
on the frayed edges
of misspelt stories.
I will not be the hesitation
that can mind me against
rebelling to a drudge's life

known to my tribe
since forever now.

Come, let's not allow it
to swallow through our plasma,
our flesh and bones,
making us a fibrous mesh
without a face, an identity!

Come, let's reach our home together!

Our Photograph

Our photo sits atop the chest
in a gilded frame
that sings of a 'Forever Love'
frozen in that one moment
when the life was new
And, I loved you
and you loved me too-
A space in a velvet moment,
A detached comfort of time.

Since then
a lot has passed by.
Life has happened,
grown old in anticipation,
lost mostly
in a tedium of monotony,
and anger,
and bitterness,
and betrayals,
the bickering arguments,

their shrapnel killed parts of me,
of you,
and sadness became
our steady visitor,
making a home with us.

Many times,
I have wanted to throw this photo
out of the window
but our children love it
and
I let it be our photograph
that the whole world sees!

Leftovers Pie

(*Ode to a Woman*)

After he's done with you,
You can
start with the remains,
a carcass.
You can start with
whatever you are left with-
shreds, broken bits or cold pieces,
even bare bones,
refrigerated, packed in ice.
Dress the wrecked flesh
in rosemary, mustard and dill,
or a riot of parsley, thyme and sage,
Marinate in a tumult of spices,
to overcome the smells of ruin,
Add butter to disparate soggy parts,
Keep in the cataclysmic heat of the oven
Golden, glossy on the cover,
cracking inside.

Presto!
Leftovers pie is ready.

Stab the center with a fork,
And enjoy once again!

Or tag
as per content-
'To Sell/ To Bin/ To Keep.'

Once again

Once again
The dragon of desire
rises from slumber
and raises its head
unleashing the flames
of longing,
of a need to fulfill
the wanton wishes,
the fervent desires,
felt in the pulsating flesh
and the deep raw core
of my woman's body.

I don't know
If I want you to douse this fire
or fan it
to make it more wild.

I left the wilderness long ago,
and have been tamed after all,

subdued into submission,
and my spirit subjugated
by the artful morality,
guarded by
the doctrines and dogmas
of this crafty world.

Words

Each new word I write,
is like rising out of
a cocoon-
a curse-
that had bound me forever
in its spindle-shaped darkness
into a nothing.

And now,
with the chrysalis shed,
I am free.

Now,
the words come out of me,
become poems,
to make me fly out
towards the sun,
to breathe the free air,
explore and experience
new feats,

caper new crusades,
raise my banner
and raid the unknown,
and know myself.

I am-
A Meaning in the Making!

www.ingramcontent.com/pod-product-compliance
Lightning Source LLC
LaVergne TN
LVHW011054200726
843509LV00011B/1404